AN OFFICIAL U.S. SPACE CAMP BOOK

THE U.S. SPACE CAMP®
BOOK OF ROCKETS

ANNE BAIRD

PHOTOGRAPHS BY
DAVID GRAHAM

FOREWORD BY
DR. BUZZ ALDRIN

INTRODUCTION BY
EDWARD O. BUCKBEE
Director, U.S. Space & Rocket Center; Founder, U.S. Space Camp

MORROW JUNIOR BOOKS · NEW YORK

*For David A., Alexander, Ashley, Joseph, Lucy, Ali, Matias, Sarah, Christopher, Rachie, Rachel,
Nicholas, Alex, Rukiya, Megan, Amanda, David S., Robert, and Simon, who always reach
for the stars, and sometimes touch them. Shine on, children!*
A.B.

Acknowledgments

Many people contributed their time, talent, energy, and resources to this book. First, Edward O. Buckbee, Director of the U.S. Space and Rocket Center and founder of U.S. Space Camp, whose enthusiasm for inspiring young people to prepare for careers of the future is so contagious; also Dr. Buzz Aldrin, whose foreword will surely encourage the next generation of space pioneers.

Richard Allen, General Manager, and Dr. Tommie R. Blackwell, Director of Education of the U.S. Space and Rocket Center, both gave invaluable assistance. Lisa Vest, Program Manager, was most helpful. A warm thank you to James Hagler, Curator of the U.S. Space and Rocket Center, and to Frederick I. Ordway, whose advice, expertise, and collection of historic space photographs added so much to this book. Thanks to all members of the Space Camp team, especially Edd Davis, Linda Burroughs, Bill Lupfer, Lisette Clemons, and counselors Danny Steele and Allyson Porterfield. Thanks also to the wonderful Space Camp trainees, who shared their excitement of learning about rockets!

We are grateful to Ken Thornsley, Charlien McGlothien, and Lisa Vasquez, who all helped us obtain crucial NASA photographs; Konrad Dannenberg, for sharing his special vision of the past and future of rocketry; and Dr. Allen E. Puckett, former Chairman of Hughes Aircraft, a much valued consultant and advisor on *The U.S. Space Camp Book of Rockets*.

Thanks also to Andrea H. Curley, our editor, who always sees the path through a maze of complex material; and to Faith Hamlin, agent extraordinaire!

No list of acknowledgments would be complete without mentioning our families, whose love and faith make everything possible.

Photo Credits

Permission to use the following photographs is gratefully acknowledged:
Frederick I. Ordway III Collection/U.S. Space and Rocket Center Archives, pages 10, 11;
Historical Division, U.S. Army Missile Command, Huntsville, Alabama, page 17 (both);
NASA, pages 1, 3, 7, 18, 19, 21, 22, 24, 31 (both), 34, 35 (both), 37, 38, 39, 43, 46;
U.S. Space and Rocket Center Archives, page 12; U.S. Space Camp/Bob Gathany, page 4.

The name SPACE CAMP is a registered trademark. Copyright © 1991
Alabama Space Science Exhibit Commission.

Design by LOGO STUDIOS/ B. Gold

Printed in the United States of America.

1 2 3 4 5 6 7 8 9 10

Library of Congress Cataloging-in-Publication Data
Baird, Anne
The U.S. Space Camp book of rockets / Anne Baird ; photographs by David Graham ;
foreword by Dr. Buzz Aldrin ; introduction by Edward O. Buckbee.
p.   cm.
Includes index.
ISBN 0-688-12228-0 (trade). — ISBN 0-688-12229-9 (lib.)
1. Rocketry—United States—History—Juvenile literature. 2. Rockets (Aeronautics)—History—Juvenile literature.
[1. Rockets (Aeronautics)—History. 2. Astronautics—History.]
I. Graham, David, ill. II. U.S. Space Camp (Huntsville, Ala.) III. Title: U.S. Space Camp book of rockets.
TL782.5.B3   1993   629.47′5—dc20   93-26148   CIP   AC

Overleaf: The space shuttle *Discovery* blasts off from Kennedy Space Center on June 6, 1990.

Foreword

As a space flyer, a spacewalker, and a moonwalker, I have had a part in fulfilling many of the dreams spawned before recorded history. The achievements of Gemini and Apollo have given a new context to the space program. The shuttle program has given birth to even more far-reaching missions and has seen world powers turn from a "space race" with one another to an enlightened spirit of cooperation for the betterment of all humankind.

There is a message as powerful as the mighty Titan II that shot the two-man Gemini capsule into space, as powerful as the awesome three-stage Saturn V that took

us to the moon. It is stunningly clear and underscores the evolution of rocketry and propulsion. We go forward because we must go; we go forward and leave a rich heritage of a proud beginning. With each passing facet of the space program we are given a renewed opportunity to dream, to reach, to inspire future generations. The tide must not be turned—the momentum must be carried by those who dare to dream, by those who seek to go forward for all humankind.

The U.S. Space Camp Book of Rockets enlightens and excites children about the future of the space program. It energizes the present generation by providing the inspiration of those space visionaries who have gone before them.

From rocket scientists, engineers, technicians, and astronauts to educators, parents, and children, the quest for space will endure.

DR. BUZZ ALDRIN
Pilot of *Gemini XII*
Lunar Module pilot of *Apollo XI*

Introduction

As director of the U.S. Space and Rocket Center in Huntsville, Alabama, for over twenty years, I have had the pleasure of working with some of the world's greatest pioneers in the history of rocketry and space. But as director of U.S. Space Camp, I am equally inspired by another group of pioneers—our future pioneers. I meet them every day at U.S. Space Camp and U.S. Space Academy. These young people come from around the globe to explore their potential as the astronauts, scientists, engineers, and educators of tomorrow. Who will be the first to set foot on Mars? Just ask our young people and they will tell you, "Me!" or "We will!"

Yes, dreams, imagination, and enthusiasm are vital characteristics of pioneers worthy to follow in the footsteps of such innovators as rocket scientist Wernher von Braun. One vital ingredient, one important link, however, is missing. The education necessary to pursue reality. While U.S. Space Camp and Academy use hands-on shuttle and space station simulations, discussions, interactive exhibits, and presentations to nurture reasoning, logic, and creativity, there must be more ways—accessible, creative ways—to effectively stimulate the desire to succeed academically.

That is why I eagerly applaud Anne Baird's involving approach to history. By combining knowledge with adventure, information with imagination, *The U.S. Space Camp Book of Rockets* provides children with a unique opportunity to immerse themselves in the history of space exploration. It dares them to accept the challenge of tomorrow's space frontier.

Inspiration, education, and determination are needed to produce a new generation of rockets, a new generation of pioneers. Lunar settlements, space farming and industry, missions to Mars, and many, many more projects await youthful vision, dreams, and commitment. Keep the dream alive. Hit the books and aim for the stars!

EDWARD O. BUCKBEE
Director, U.S. Space and Rocket Center
Founder, U.S. Space Camp

Contents

HOW IT ALL BEGAN

9:57 A.M. The heat on the roof of the Astronaut Hall of Fame, just 10 miles away from the Kennedy Space Center in Florida, is 90°F and climbing. But nobody thinks of returning to the air-conditioned building.

Atlantis, going on America's forty-ninth shuttle mission, is scheduled for launch in a matter of seconds. Not one of the 260 Space Camp trainees packed on the roof of the Florida camp would miss it. Neither would the people crammed around them and on the lawn below, or the thousands more standing on the hoods of their campers and cars along the roads leading to the launch site.

The only sound is from the intercom system on the observation deck, broadcasting the countdown from Launch Pad 39B.

"Five...four...three...two...one..."

Suddenly a blaze of light flashes against the sky. *Atlantis*'s three main engines and two solid-fuel rocket boosters ignite and roar into life. They push the 4.5-million-pound shuttle off the launch pad and hurl it skyward.

"WE HAVE LIFT-OFF!"

The Space Camp trainees see *Atlantis* before they hear it: a silent, gleaming cylinder soaring into space atop a pillar of smoke and fire. Fifty seconds later the noise reaches their ears.

Then it hits: a popping crackle that quickly swells into a storm of sound and vibrates the concrete beneath their feet. The shuttle's thunder is so enormous that it is heard and felt 20 miles from the launch site.

Now the trainees scream. They jump. They cheer. *Atlantis* is disappearing fast.

Only a trail of smoke, breaking up in the wind, marks its path.

"Did you see those rockets?" a trainee asks, struggling to put the experience into words. "The way they looked against the sky? Awesome!"

Another trainee grins. "No rockets, no lift-off," he says. "We can't get into space without 'em...."

At Space Camp in Huntsville, Alabama, counselor Danny Steele tucks a red balloon into his shorts pocket as he leads his group of trainees, the Apple team, outside to launch their homemade two-stage rockets. When they reach the launch field, Danny will load a small engine into each rocket. A solid propellant, or fuel, will propel the rocket. When it is ignited, the rocket will shoot up.

Like the children's rockets, the space shuttle also launches when its engines and solid-fuel rocket boosters are ignited. Why?

Danny talks about it as he kneels in the grass and gathers his team around him. "What's the name of the law that tells how rockets work?" he asks.

"Newton's Third Law of Motion," says one trainee.

"Yes! What does it say?"

"For every action there is an equal and opposite reaction!" yells the team.

"Right!" Danny shouts back.

To demonstrate what that means, he pulls the balloon out of his pocket, blows it up, then sets it free. "Blast off!" he yells.

Counselor Danny Steele demonstrates Newton's Third Law of Motion using a red balloon.

As the compressed air rushes out of the balloon's opening—the "action"—the balloon shoots off in the opposite direction—the "reaction." It whizzes around until it's empty, then falls to the ground.

"Think of a rocket as the red balloon," Danny explains. "The balloon is pushed forward when the mass of air I blew into it escapes. A rocket has propellants inside it.

"When the propellant is ignited, gases shoot out of the rocket nozzle. That makes the rocket fly in the opposite direction until all its propellant is spent. Then, like the empty balloon, the rocket returns to Earth. Now, let's see how *your* rockets do," he finishes.

Members of the Apple team launch their two-stage rockets.

The rocket launches go well. Only one fizzles. The almost-perfect launch is a tribute to the care the young rocketeers have taken.

"Good job!" Danny tells the jubilant team. "Tomorrow we'll tour the Rocket Park and learn a little rocket history. Humans shot into space in the second half of the twentieth century. But dreams of space travel came first—in myths, poems, art, and science fiction. Some of those ideas seem pretty weird today. But those crazy dreams led to the Space Age...."

DREAMS TO REALITIES: EARLY ROCKETS

The Apple team walks to the Rocket Park on the grounds of the Space and Rocket Center, where Space Camp is located. Along the way, Danny talks. "Early dreams of flight are shared by many cultures," he begins. "The ancient Greeks had a story about a boy named Icarus, who flew with wings made of feathers. Other early stories of flight used birds, demons, spirits, horses, winds, and even thoughts to transport space travelers."

"Didn't anybody think of rockets?"

"Not for quite a long time," answers Danny. "But by the seventeenth century people knew more about science. Authors began using scientific-sounding devices in their stories: antigravity machines, magnets, bottles of evaporating dew, and balloons. This kind of story is called science fiction.

"Jules Verne was the most famous science-fiction writer of the nineteenth century. He was the first to have his astronauts travel to the moon in a rocket-like spaceship. But even though he knew about rockets, he didn't dream of using one to *launch* his spacecraft. In his book *From the Earth to the Moon*, the ship was shot out of a cannon! Still, Verne was a great writer. He made space travel seem possible. Several of his ideas, such as weightlessness in space, proved true. And his books inspired many of the founders of modern spaceflight."

"Who made the first rockets?" asks one of the children.

"Probably the Chinese," says Danny.

"They discovered explosive 'black powder'—which we know as gunpowder—sometime in the tenth century. By the thirteenth century they were packing the powder into tubes and shooting rocket-powered 'fire arrows' at their enemies. Wars and trade spread their technology to most of Asia and Europe. In Europe, though, rockets were used mostly for fireworks displays. But all that changed in 1792."

"Why?"

"War," says Danny. "An Indian prince, Tippoo Sultan, successfully fought the British army at a place called Seringapatam using rockets. The rockets were iron tubes filled with gunpowder and attached to long bamboo guiding sticks. The rocketeer lit the fuse and aimed the rocket at the enemy.

"After Seringapatam more armies used rockets as weapons; but they were so inaccurate that by the end of the nineteenth century, they were replaced by new, improved weapons such as rifles and cannons.

"During World War I, from 1914 to 1918, rockets were used for signaling, lighting up enemy positions, and laying smoke screens. Still, they were not regarded as a major weapon.

"When World War II started in 1939, however, the rocket finally came into its own. Germany's V-2 rocket saw to that...."

In the eleventh century, the Persian poet Firdausi wrote about a king who flew to the moon on a throne harnessed to four hungry eagles *(opposite)*. The eagles flew forward, trying to get to the meat just beyond their reach. In the nineteenth century, Jules Verne's book *From the Earth to the Moon* told of an imaginary flight to the moon in a rocketlike capsule 104 years before human beings actually landed there *(right)*.

The V-2

The Deadly Rocket of World War II

In the Rocket Park, the children look up at a V-2 rocket. Compared to other rockets in the park, the V-2 is tiny. Standing just 46.1 feet tall, it weighs only 12.25 tons.

"Looks like a prop in a Buck Rogers movie, doesn't it?" says Danny. "But it was deadly. If Adolf Hitler had developed it sooner, the Allies might have lost the war."

During World War II, scientists on both sides of the conflict worked hard to create rocket-powered weapons for their armies. The German team, led by Wernher von Braun, was very successful. They created the V-2. This rocket could reach a target 200 miles away in five minutes. Its guidance system, composed of three gyroscopes, made it more accurate, and dangerous, than any other weapon at that time. Toward the end of the war, in 1944, a hail of V-2 rockets bombed England and Belgium daily. Thousands died.

When the victorious Allies invaded Germany, von Braun and 120 members of his team surrendered to the Americans. The Soviet Union, the English, and the French captured other German engineers, whom they later used to develop their own rocket programs. In 1945 von Braun

Wernher von Braun helped create the V-2 and later aided the United States in developing rockets that sent the first men to the moon.

and some of his team were taken to the United States. With them went 90 V-2s and spare parts. The team signed up as rocket consultants to the American army!

At the U.S. Army's White Sands Proving Grounds in New Mexico, they helped the Americans assemble and launch the V-2s. In this way the United States learned vital rocket technology.

Wernher von Braun was a scientist. During the war he had wanted to build rockets for space travel, not destruction. And after the war his heart was still set on space exploration. But as soon as World War II was over, a new "war" began: the Cold War between the United States and its former ally, the Soviet Union (U.S.S.R.). A race to conquer space, and to build bigger missiles, began. To win this competition, America needed more powerful rocket launchers.

Konrad Dannenberg, one of the original members of von Braun's team and now a speaker at the Huntsville Space Camp, stands beside one of these deadly rockets of World War II.

In 1950 von Braun and his team, including an engineer named Konrad Dannenberg, moved to the U.S. Army's Redstone Arsenal in Huntsville, Alabama—only a few miles away from where Space Camp is now located. Here they helped design the rockets the United States needed for defense.

The Redstone Rocket
The Missile That Became Peaceful

"**O**n August 20, 1953, von Braun and his men launched the Redstone rocket," Danny informs Apple team. "It was named after the place where it was developed."

The Redstone was an upgraded version of the V-2. Its range and payload, or the amount of equipment it could carry, were no greater than that of its famous predecessor. But its engine was more reliable than the V-2's, and it was the first rocket to have a peaceful as well as a military use.

As a space-exploration rocket, it launched the first U.S. manned suborbital flights during the Mercury program. Eventually it became the first rocket stage, or section of larger two- and three-stage rockets, that launched satellites and unmanned probes.

As a medium-range ballistic missile launcher, it could fire warheads at a target 200 miles away, traveling 3,800 miles per hour. After it is launched, a ballistic missile flies through space with no guidance system—like a baseball once it has been thrown by the pitcher. So Redstone was not accurate enough or powerful enough to launch satellites or space capsules into orbit. A new launcher was needed to do that.

The U.S. government chose the Navy's three-stage Vanguard rocket to launch America's first satellite, *Explorer I*. Vanguard was based on Viking rockets, which had launched a series of scientific probes of Earth's atmosphere.

Von Braun's three-stage Jupiter-C rocket, developed with the U.S. Army, used the Redstone missile launcher as its first stage. Officials decided that peaceful space exploration should be carried out by rockets developed for scientific purposes instead of military rockets. So Jupiter-C was passed over!

Juno II and the Redstone rocket are neighbors in the Rocket Park.

Juno I

America's First Successful Space Rocket

"**O**n October 4, 1957, America received a terrible shock," Danny continues. "The Soviet Union was first into space."

With the launch of *Sputnik I*, a 184-pound Soviet satellite that circled Earth every 96 minutes, the world entered the Space Age. A month later the Soviets scored again. They launched an even bigger satellite, *Sputnik II*. Aboard was a dog named Laika—the first living creature in space.

And if the United States was discouraged then, it was even more so on December 6. The Vanguard rocket, which was supposed to launch the first U.S. satellite, blew up one second after lift-off in front of a worldwide TV audience.

Wernher von Braun was asked to launch another satellite by March of 1958. He beat the deadline. On January 31, 1958, the 36-pound, 6.7-foot-long *Explorer I* was launched successfully from Cape Canaveral, Florida. It soared into space atop Juno I, a Jupiter-C rocket with a fourth stage. Juno I's four rocket stages were mounted on top of one another. The first rocket carried the upper stages to a high altitude until its propellant was burned up. Then it separated and fell away. This lightened the rocket so it could go farther and faster. The same thing happened to the second and third stages. The last stage, a rocket attached to *Explorer I*, shot it into orbit. This multistage principle was an important breakthrough in rocket technology that is still used today.

Explorer beat *Sputnik*'s record of 92 days in orbit by staying in space until March 31, 1970. It transmitted important scientific data for four months. However, this U.S. victory was surpassed by the launch of the Soviet Union's *Sputnik III* on May 15.

Americans were alarmed by this dramatic evidence that the U.S.S.R. was becoming an economic and technological superpower. The government feared that the United States might lose its Number One position. Something had to be done!

On July 29, 1958, President Dwight D. Eisenhower formed the National Aeronautics and Space Administration (NASA) to take control of all peaceful space activities in the country. NASA's first project was the Mercury program.

"Mercury was a program to put a man into orbit, observe his reactions, and recover him safely," says Danny. "From then on, most of NASA's time and money were spent trying to put human beings into space.

"The program was a success. From 1958 to 1963, NASA made twenty-five test and flight missions, using twenty spacecraft, twenty-four launch rockets, four animals, and six astronauts. And not a single animal or human was lost!

"For the program, NASA chose America's first astronauts. They were called the Mercury Seven."

THE MERCURY PROGRAM

Jupiter

Launcher of America's Monkeynauts

Apple team moves to the Army's Jupiter rocket. Danny tells them about it. "America's first astronauts weren't chosen from the Mercury Seven after all. They were monkeys: an American-born rhesus named Able and a South American squirrel monkey named Miss Baker. Able was a last-minute replacement for an Indian rhesus. Monkeys are sacred to some Indian people, and officials didn't want to offend anybody."

The monkeys were launched first because NASA needed to verify that living creatures could survive launch and recovery before it risked the lives of the astronauts.

The Rocket Park is home to many famous rockets. From left to right you can see Jupiter, Juno II, the Redstone rocket, Mercury-Redstone, and Jupiter C.

NASA used a Jupiter ballistic missile developed by the Army with von Braun's help. Technicians modified it for the monkeys' mission by replacing its military warhead with a special container for the animals. Able and Miss Baker were strapped into the nose cone. Sensors monitored their response to the stresses of their flight.

The two monkeys blasted off from Cape Canaveral on May 28, 1959. During their wild ride they reached speeds of up to 10,000 miles per hour. They traveled 300 miles high and 1,500 miles out over the Atlantic Ocean. When their capsule splashed down 15 minutes later, its descent slowed by a reentry parachute, both monkeys were recovered alive!

Able died shortly after his flight from a non-space-related infection. But Miss Baker lived fifteen years longer—at the U.S. Space and Rocket Center. Every year of her life, trainees celebrated her birthday with a party.

Like the Russian cosmodog Laika before them, these monkeys proved that living creatures could survive in space. The stage was finally set for America's first manned flight aboard the Mercury-Redstone rocket!

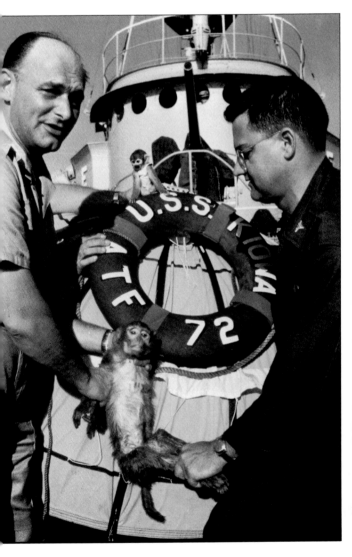

Miss Baker, perched on the U.S.S. *Kiowa*'s life preserver, and her companion, Able, pose for the photographers *(left)*. They have just been picked up from the Atlantic Ocean, where their capsule parachuted safely after their historic flight in 1959. Both animals are alive and well! Later occupants of Miss Baker's former cage at the Space and Rocket Center excite the Apple team's interest *(below)*. Miss Baker lived in this cage for fifteen years after her flight. She never flew again but was taken on occasional outings by her keepers. The museum no longer has the cage or the monkeys.

The Mercury-Redstone

Rocket Booster for America's First Manned Spaceflight

The children look up at Mercury-Redstone. It's beautiful. Tall, slender, gleaming white with black-and-white stripes, it looks as if it could leap into the sky at any minute. It is topped by a red-painted rescue tower. Rockets attached to the tower could be fired to separate the capsule from the launch rocket if it exploded right after liftoff. The rescue tower was supposed to give the astronaut a chance to escape in case of disaster.

Danny consults his notes.

"Mercury-Redstone was a stretched version of the Redstone ballistic missile. The height of the rocket, including the spacecraft on top, was 83 feet; it weighed 33 tons."

"How many stages did it have?" asks a trainee.

"One," answers Danny. "NASA didn't want to put an astronaut into orbit without first finding out how humans responded to launch and recovery. Because of that, the Mercury-Redstone, with its limited power, was the perfect rocket. It could loft capsules only into suborbital flight. That means that the capsule couldn't go high enough or fast enough to keep circling Earth. It came down quickly once its fuel was used up.

"But the Soviets beat America again. On April 12, 1961, less than a month before a U.S. astronaut was scheduled to go up, cosmonaut Yuri A. Gagarin became the first man in space. He made a 1-hour, 48-minute orbit around Earth."

"I wish we'd been first," says another trainee.

Danny laughs. "So did a lot of Americans," he says. "But the important thing is that space exploration raced ahead *because* of the competition between America and the U.S.S.R. Another important thing is that the United States didn't quit."

The six-story-high Mercury-Redstone rocket finally launches on May 5, 1961, at 9:34 A.M. after an agonizing four-hour delay. Fifteen minutes later, the historic flight is over.

After he was recovered from the Atlantic Ocean, America's first man in space, Alan Shepard, declared that his five minutes of weightlessness were "just a pleasant ride."

On May 5, 1961, the United States finally launched its first manned flight. Mercury-Redstone shot Commander Alan B. Shepard, Jr., in *Freedom VII*, to an altitude of 115 miles. He streaked 302 miles down the Atlantic Missile Range, the stretch of ocean off Cape Canaveral. He reached a speed of 5,200 miles per hour before splashing down by parachute.

The flight lasted only 15 minutes. But it was historic! Although monkeys had survived spaceflight, NASA could not be sure how an astronaut's body would react to the stresses of spaceflight. The rocket launcher might even explode! Because of these fears, the Mercury capsule was designed to fly on automatic pilot in case the astronaut couldn't function.

Astronauts who flew inside these spacecraft were crammed into an area about the size of a phone booth. The craft was packed with instruments and retro-rockets that slowed its entry into Earth's atmosphere. Limited space was the main reason early astronauts could be no taller than 5 feet 11 inches, or weigh more than 180 pounds.

Commander Shepard's mission was to survive, to evaluate his response to rocket-powered flight, and to test the spacecraft's controls, if he were able. He performed his mission flawlessly and returned a hero.

Twenty days later and after only 15 minutes of American manned spaceflight experience, America's new president, John F. Kennedy, made a stunning announcement: The United States would land a man on the moon, and return him safely to Earth, by 1970. Overnight, the race between the U.S.S.R. and the U.S.A. was hotter than ever!

After Mercury-Redstone launched Virgil I. "Gus" Grissom into a second suborbital flight on July 21, NASA decided no more such flights were needed. The Redstone rocket was out of a job. A more powerful rocket, Atlas, launched the remaining Mercury missions into orbital flight.

Mercury-Atlas

The Missile That Launched America's First Orbital Flight

Danny now takes the team to see Atlas, lying on its side in the Rocket Park. "This was America's first intercontinental ballistic missile," he begins. "An ICBM has a range of 3,500 to 4,000 miles. It can travel from one continent to another and is powerful enough to put a human into Earth orbit.

"Starting in 1959, NASA adapted the Atlas missile for various space programs. It was used to launch a series of unmanned probes. Even today it's used to launch scientific probes and satellites. The Mercury program's version of this famous missile orbited six missions. Four of them were manned."

The capsule weighed 1.9 tons at liftoff. Shaped like an ice-cream cone with its point cut off, it carried smaller rockets that performed various jobs during flight. Eighteen of these rockets allowed the astronaut to control Mercury's position. Three other rockets were used to separate the capsule from the launch rocket, and three more to return it home from orbit.

On November 29, 1961, a final test flight of Mercury-Atlas was flown, carrying a chimpanzee named Enos. Three months later, on February 20, 1962, astronaut John H. Glenn, Jr., piloted the first American orbital flight aboard *Mercury-Atlas VI*.

Glenn made three complete orbits of Earth, easily operating the capsule's controls. Splashdown went off perfectly, and

Three Rocket Park giants, Mercury-Redstone, Atlas, and Saturn V, gleam in the hot Alabama sun. The silver military version of Atlas was modified to become Mercury-Atlas, the rocket that lofted John Glenn into America's first orbital flight on February 20, 1962.

he came home to ticker tape parades and fame.

NASA had hoped that Glenn's orbital flight would help America catch up with the Soviet Union. It didn't. On August 6, 1961, months before Glenn's mission, cosmonaut Gherman S. Titov had orbited Earth 16 times in 25 hours. He was the first man to spend a day in outer space.

Still NASA went on. Three more Mercury astronauts—M. Scott Carpenter, Walter M. Schirra, and L. Gordon Cooper—were launched into orbital flight over the next 15 months. Their missions helped close the gap in the space race and advanced NASA's understanding of the problems and requirements of space travel.

NASA now felt it had learned all it could from the Mercury program, and it came to an end.

John Glenn eases into his molded-to-fit couch in the Mercury capsule *Friendship VII*. During his three-orbit flight he reported seeing a mass of brightly lit particles flying past the capsule that "look like little stars!"

"Project Mercury was NASA's first step in a three-step plan to land astronauts on the moon," says Danny. "Mercury taught NASA that humans could survive and perform in a space environment. Basic space technology and hardware were developed, and a pool of astronauts was trained. It was time to move on to step two: the Gemini program.

"Gemini was named for the twin stars, and the spacecraft carried *two* astronauts into space. The purpose of this program was to keep astronauts in space for longer periods and to let them practice the orbiting, rendezvousing, and docking maneuvers that would be needed to make a landing on the moon.

"Do you all know what those last two terms mean?" Danny asks his team.

"Of course," says a Space Camp trainee, nodding her head. "'Rendezvousing' is when astronauts pilot their craft to a certain place in space, where they meet another spaceship. 'Docking' is when the two spacecraft link up so that crew members can cross over from one ship to the other."

"A Gemini spacecraft must have been bigger and heavier than a Mercury," says another trainee thoughtfully.

"It was," replies Danny, "and to launch it, NASA needed a more powerful rocket. It chose Titan II."

THE GEMINI PROGRAM

Gemini-Titan II

The Rocket That Helped America Win the Space Race

Danny shows the team a photograph of Titan II and gives them some background about it.

"In the early sixties, the U.S.S.R. continued its string of space firsts: the first rendezvous in space in 1962; the first woman in space, Valentina V. Tereshkova, in 1963; the first three-person team into orbit in 1964; and the first spacewalk in 1965.

"After that last Soviet victory, American spaceflights increased dramatically. During the Gemini program, from March 23, 1965, to November 15, l966, only one Soviet rocket was launched. America's Titan launched ten successful manned flights! This paved the way for the next step in the U.S. space program."

The children study the picture of Titan II. It was a two-stage rocket, standing 103 feet tall with its warhead. Both stages were 10 feet in diameter. Including propellants, the rocket weighed about 150 tons. In tests it flew faster than 15,000 miles per hour. It had the power to launch the 3.6-ton Gemini capsule.

"The U.S. Air Force developed Titan II in 1964," says Danny. "At the time it was the free world's most powerful ICBM. Like Atlas, this missile was adapted by NASA to launch unmanned space probes and manned spacecraft. It was the rocket that finally helped America catch up with the Soviet Union. Later versions of it are still used for unmanned launches today."

We have lift-off! *Gemini VIII*, the sixth manned Gemini mission powered by Titan II, rockets aloft on March 16, 1966. Astronauts Neil Armstrong and David Scott's mission was to rendezvous and dock with an Agena target vehicle in space. They succeeded but returned to Earth early when a rocket thruster malfunctioned, causing the capsule to spin wildly in space.

The Apple team looks at the one-man Mercury Procedures capsule in which Mercury astronauts trained (below), and then at the two-man, open-hatched Gemini capsule containing a pair of couches (right). According to astronaut Gus Grissom, who helped design it, Gemini looked "like a Mercury capsule that threw the diet rules away." It had 50 percent more cabin space than Mercury and weighed more than twice as much—about 8,000 pounds.

Now Apple team goes to the Space and Rocket Center's museum, where the children look at a Gemini capsule. It has Mercury's bulletlike look, but it is very different inside.

Gemini's two-man crew sat in a roomier cockpit, with controls, instrument panels, and ejection seats like a military aircraft. And the Gemini capsule had rocket engines to change its orbital path, radar to help astronauts rendezvous with other space vehicles, and a fuel cell to provide electricity for longer missions. Like the Mercury capsule, a Gemini craft depended upon parachutes to slow its descent into the ocean.

The Gemini program's first manned flight took place on March 23, 1965. Gus Grissom and John W. Young flew three orbits in *Gemini III*, altering their orbital path by using the capsule's rocket thrusters.

"A series of American firsts followed," says Danny, leading his team onward.

During the *Gemini IV* mission of June 3-7, 1965, Astronaut Edward H. White made America's first tethered spacewalk. Attached by an umbilical cord to the spacecraft, he moved by firing a hand-held, gas-filled rocket gun.

During the next eight Gemini missions, astronauts orbited Earth for longer periods. They practiced the rendezvousing, docking, and spacewalk procedures they would use during lunar flights and landings.

Gemini VII, piloted by astronauts Frank Borman and James A. Lovell, Jr., was NASA's longest mission to date—206 orbits, or two weeks in space. During the mission, Borman and Lovell's craft rendezvoused with *Gemini VI*, piloted by Schirra and Thomas P. Stafford. This was the first American rendezvous between two manned space vehicles. The two craft came within one foot of each other! The first space docking took place on March 15, 1966: Neil A. Armstrong and David R. Scott linked up their *Gemini VIII* capsule with an Agena rocket stage.

With the last three Gemini missions, *X*, *XI*, and *XII*, each performing a successful rendezvous, docking, and spacewalk, it was time to move on to the third and last phase of the lunar landing program: Apollo.

"The ten manned Gemini missions were a great success. They proved that astronauts could survive and operate in space for at least two weeks. This was the maximum time NASA thought a lunar mission would take," says Danny. "NASA learned that one spacecraft could find another and dock with it. Best of all, astronaut and flight control crews gained experience. NASA was ready to start on Project Apollo—the three-man mission to the moon. What did they need for that?"

"A new spacecraft?" says a trainee.

"Yes..."

"And a bigger rocket!" yells the team.

"You got it," says Danny. "To get to the moon, the U.S. needed to build the biggest rocket the world had ever seen. It was called Saturn. Let's see it."

Tethered to his *Gemini IV* capsule by a 25-foot cord providing oxygen and two-way communication with the spacecraft, Edward White takes America's first spacewalk on June 3, 1965. In his left hand is the Hand-Held Self-Maneuvering Unit that he fired in bursts to move around the spacecraft. When time ran out and he had to return to *Gemini* after 21 minutes in space, he said, "It's the saddest moment of my life."

THE APOLLO PROGRAM

Saturn I

The First American Rocket Designed Just for Space Exploration

Back outside, the children look up—way up—at Saturn I. "This two-stage rocket was the first space vehicle designed just for space exploration," says Danny.

"Saturn, like the Apollo program itself, was developed a step at a time. The rocket you are looking at was the first of three Saturns—each one more powerful than the other. All three were developed under the leadership of Wernher von Braun at NASA's Marshall Space Flight Center right here in Huntsville. Its purpose was to prepare the way to send astronauts to the moon."

Saturn I towers over the cluster of free-standing rockets in the Rocket Park.

The von Braun team began by using ideas they had developed earlier. Saturn I was made of eight Redstone-type propellant tanks clustered around a Jupiter tank. The first stage of the rocket was powered by eight Jupiter engines.

Saturn I, launched on October 27, 1961, could place 11 tons of weight into Earth orbit. It was nearly 190 feet tall and weighed about 514 tons when fully loaded with liquid fuel. Between 1961 and 1965, nine Saturn I vehicles were successfully launched. Saturn I also launched the first unmanned Apollo spacecraft, as well as three Pegasus satellites. These satellites were designed to study problems caused by meteors striking spacecraft, and were useful to NASA engineers who were developing the Apollo spacecraft for the moon flight.

Then came Saturn IB.

Saturn IB

Launcher of *Apollo VII,* the Skylab Astronauts, and the Apollo-Soyuz Test Project

"**S**aturn IB was an upgraded version of Saturn I," quotes Danny, reading from his notebook. "The two-stage rocket stood 225 feet tall and weighed about 582 tons when fully loaded. It was scheduled to launch the first manned Apollo mission into space. But *Apollo I* never got off the launch pad."

On January 27, 1967, a flash fire broke out in the *Apollo I* capsule during a pre-flight training mission. Tragically, astronauts Grissom, White, and Roger Chaffee died in the inferno.

For nearly two years afterward, while NASA worked to improve the space capsule, only unmanned Apollo missions were launched. Saturn IB finally boosted the improved *Apollo VII* and astronauts Schirra, Donn F. Eisele, and R. Walter Cunningham into Earth orbit on October 11, 1968.

Saturn IB went on to launch three Skylab missions in 1973. Skylab, the world's first orbiting space station, had been boosted into Earth orbit on May 14, 1973, by a Saturn V rocket. Eleven days later a Saturn IB rocket propelled its first crew to their temporary house-sized home in space. During their stays the astronauts performed extravehicular activities (EVAs) in the void of space, carried out experiments in the lab—and proved that humans could survive and work in the space environment for at least three months, the length of the longest stay.

Unfortunately, Skylab's orbit deteriorated over seven years, and it sank lower and lower over Earth. The parts of it that were not consumed by its fiery entry into Earth's atmosphere fell harmlessly to the ground in a sparsely populated section of Australia. The largest part of it to be found is on exhibit at the U.S. Space and Rocket Center.

On July 15, 1975, Saturn IB ended its career by launching the Apollo-Soyuz Test Project. This Apollo spacecraft, with astronauts Stafford, Vance Brand, and Donald "Deke" Slayton aboard, rendezvoused and docked with a U.S.S.R. Soyuz spacecraft carrying cosmonauts Alexei Leonov and Valery Kubasov. The two capsules remained linked for 44 hours. For that brief period the spacemen set aside their countries' rivalry as they shared friendship, food, and scientific experiments. Their mission affirmed the need for peaceful cooperation in space between spacefaring nations.

"Saturn IB's career as a rocket launcher spanned such a long period of time that we're getting ahead of ourselves," says Danny. "We'd better back up to 1968—and the race to the moon.

"With the success of *Apollo VII,* NASA moved to step three. Saturn V, the most powerful rocket ever built, was designed to loft a crew of three to the moon!"

Saturn V
The Moon Rocket

The mighty Saturn V lies on its side in the Rocket Park. It is pulled apart into its three stages, including the *Apollo* spacecraft, so visitors can examine it. Even lying on the ground the rocket is awesome. Close by stands a huge F-1 engine.

"There were five of those engines on the first stage alone," says Danny, boosting a trainee into one of the engines to give the team an idea of its monstrous size.

"We could fit *three* teams into one of these things," yells the boy. "Maybe more."

The huge three-stage rocket, with the *Apollo* capsule riding on top, stood 363 feet tall. It was bigger than a 29-story skyscraper! At lift-off it weighed more than 3,000 tons. Most of that weight was the 2,948 tons of rocket propellant. The rocket needed every ounce of that fuel to pull away from Earth's gravity and to set *Apollo* on course for the moon.

The first manned flight to the moon, launched by Saturn V, was on December 21, 1968. Astronauts Borman, Lovell, and William A. Anders made ten lunar orbits, but they did not land. However, they did transmit pictures of what they saw to Earth. For the first time millions of people all over the world saw the stark, lifeless moonscape on TV. More than seven months would pass, and three more lunar flights would take place, before NASA was ready to land astronauts on its bleak surface.

A Space Camp trainee poses in one of Saturn V's five engines to show its enormous size. These engines, which powered Apollo's first stage only, were designed to generate 160 million horsepower—or the equivalent of 86 Hoover Dams!

How long does it take to race 363 feet? Apple team tries to find out by running the length of Saturn V.

The children race the length of Saturn. When they reach the end, Danny tells them about the different pieces they've passed.

"Stage one is 138 feet long and 33 feet wide. Each of its five F-1 engines consumed 5,000 gallons of liquid propellant a second. The engines generated 7.6 million pounds of thrust to lift the rocket off the ground. The roar of the rocket engines was louder than 8 million stereos turned up to maximum volume."

In 2.5 minutes, the first stage consumed most of its propellants. It reached a speed of 6,000 miles per hour at a height of 35 miles above Earth. At this point the first stage shut down and fell into the Atlantic Ocean.

Then the second stage fired. The thrust of its engines shot the spacecraft to 108 miles above Earth. When its propellant was exhausted, stage two separated from the rocket and plunged into the Indian Ocean.

Next, the third stage fired, boosting it and the *Apollo* capsule into Earth orbit. After one to three orbits, the stage's engines fired again to push the stage, including the *Apollo* capsule, out of Earth orbit. *Apollo* was on its way to the moon and Saturn V's job was done. The crew in *Apollo*'s command module docked with and disengaged their lunar module from the third stage of the Saturn V rocket. That stage was abandoned. It either burned up in space or, in some missions, crashed onto the surface of the moon. The astronauts continued their journey in the *Apollo* spacecraft.

"The trip from Earth to the moon took three days and nights," says Danny. "Once there, only the astronauts' skill and the reliability of their vehicle could bring them safely home again.

"There were eleven manned Apollo missions between 1968 and 1972, and six lunar landings. NASA didn't lose a single Apollo astronaut or spacecraft in all that time. It's incredible!"

"Let's go see the museum's Apollo collection," says one of the trainees.

Members of the Apple team try out Space Camp's Apollo Mission Simulator. It's fun to see how it felt to be an Apollo astronaut. "Squished!" reports a trainee.

The children are excited by the Apollo spacecraft. Apollo had three main stages: the command module, the service module, and the two-part lunar lander. The U.S. Space and Rocket Center has a real Apollo command module, a training command module, and a model of the complete lunar lander.

The team examines the *Apollo XVI* capsule that carried astronauts Young, Thomas K. Mattingly II, and Charles M. Duke to the moon in 1972. They climb into the training command module of the three-man spacecraft to see how it felt to be an Apollo astronaut.

"I'm squished!" says a trainee, working the switches on the control panels above his horizontal couch. "How did the astronauts take it for over eight days?"

"Only the astronauts who stayed in the module had to," says another. "Twelve Apollo astronauts got to stretch their legs on the moon."

On July 16, 1969, *Apollo XI* launched from the Kennedy Space Center. Four days later the dreams of Icarus and of others like him came true. Neil Armstrong and Buzz Aldrin flew down to a new world. They traveled in a spiderlike, metal, two-part lunar lander named for a noble bird—the *Eagle*.

Astronaut Michael Collins stayed in the command module, named *Columbia*, and continued to orbit the moon.

For two-and-a-half hours the astronauts hopped around in the lunar gravity in which they weighed only one-sixth of their Earth weight. After planting an American flag in the powdery gray soil, they set up a seismometer to record moonquakes and meteor hits. They collected dirt and rock samples. Then they reboarded the top part of *Eagle*, the ascent module, fired its rockets, and returned to the command module. *Eagle*'s landing stage was left on the moon.

Topped by the launch escape tower, *Apollo XI* soars aloft on a column of fire as it blasts off from Kennedy Space Center at 9:32 A.M., July 16, 1969 *(left)*. Its mission: to land the first men on the moon! The second man to walk on the moon, astronaut Buzz Aldrin, descends the steps of the Lunar Module's ladder as he prepares to walk on the moon *(right)*.

Once docked with the command module, the astronauts released the ascent module and returned to Earth in the command capsule. Splashdown in the ocean was slowed, as always, by the capsule's reentry parachutes. *Apollo* had three of them.

NASA beat President Kennedy's deadline for sending Americans to the moon by five months. *Apollo*'s triumph made America first in space at last!

In all, the mighty Saturn V rockets launched thirteen missions, six of them resulting in actual lunar landings. The greatest launch of all was the one that placed the first man on the moon.

As the Apple team ends its investigation of the Apollo spacecraft, Danny sums up an era in space history. "The Apollo moon program, powered by Saturn rockets, ended in 1972. But images of those astronauts walking on the moon will always be with us. The twentieth century will be remembered as the time when human beings first left their home on Earth. After that, nothing would seem truly impossible."

THE SPACE SHUTTLE

Returning to their dorms to get ready for lunch, the team crosses Shuttle Park and passes beneath *Pathfinder*, a full-scale model of the space shuttle. It was originally used by NASA at both the Marshall Space Flight Center and the Kennedy Space Center to learn how to transport a huge shuttle from the assembly building to the launch pad. Now it stands in the Space and Rocket Center's park.

In the shimmering noon heat *Pathfinder*'s shadow on the pavement looks cool and

Pathfinder, Space Camp's full-scale model of the space shuttle, dominates Shuttle Park.

inviting. The children stop and look up. The gleaming white shuttle, perched on top of its gigantic orange-colored external tank, resembles a jetliner. Attached to the sides of the external tank are two solid rocket boosters.

Poised on its concrete pillars, *Pathfinder* seems ready to leap from its moorings and follow *Columbia, Challenger, Discovery, Atlantis,* and *Endeavour* into space.

Danny tells the team about the program that created these enormous space launchers. "As the Apollo project ended, NASA made plans for the future. Committed to the idea of manned space exploration, they wanted to build a new space station to replace Skylab."

It would be different. It would be a permanently manned orbiting station for scientific research. To get to and from it, NASA and its aerospace contractors would develop a reusable spacecraft.

The space station program began in January 1984, when President Ronald Reagan announced it in his State of the Union address. The station, named Freedom, has been in the planning stages ever since. The huge cost of developing, building, and orbiting Freedom in space has delayed its construction.

Since manned space exploration is so expensive, no nation can hope to go it alone anymore. Because of this, NASA, for the first time, has formed an alliance with some of the world's new spacefaring nations. Canada, Japan, and several European countries have agreed to help build Freedom. The combined resources of many nations will be needed if complex projects like this are to come about. Russia, the former head of the Soviet Union, with its long history as a pioneer in space, will probably continue to play a role.

Freedom has been delayed. But the space transportation program is going strong. The reusable spacecraft—the space shuttle—is already built and in use.

This huge flying machine is presently being used for three main jobs. First, it is an orbiting space laboratory. Second, it carries and launches scientific equipment into low Earth orbit. Third, it houses crews that do important work: They perform experiments, capture damaged satellites in orbit and either repair them in space or bring them back to Earth to be fixed. Once Freedom is constructed, the shuttle is expected to ferry astronauts and materials back and forth between it and Earth, like a bus.

Solid rocket boosters blazing, *Atlantis*, the United States's fourth orbiter vehicle, blasts into space on October 3, 1985. First, the orbiter's three main engines fire. Next, the solid rocket boosters ignite. Finally, the two orbital maneuvering system engines, located just above the two bottom main engines, fire and put the spacecraft into Earth orbit.

The space shuttle is partly reusable. It has three main parts: the orbiter; the external tank (ET); and the two solid-rocket booster motors (SRBMs).

The orbiter carries the crew and payload, and is used over and over again. Powered by three liquid-propellant engines located at its base, it also has two orbital maneuvering system (OMS) rockets that place it in Earth orbit and later take it out of orbit for return to Earth.

The white SRBMs, attached to the sides of the ET, each carry 500 tons of solid propellant that provides extra thrust for the fiery lift-off and ascent of the shuttle. Two minutes after lift-off, the propellant is all burned up. The boosters separate from the ET and fall into the Atlantic Ocean. There they are quickly located, thanks to their brightly colored reentry parachutes. A ship picks them up, and they are made ready for another flight.

The ET is loaded with 526,616 gallons of liquid hydrogen and oxygen for the shuttle's three main rocket engines. This fuel is used up less than ten minutes after lift-off. When the ET is nearly empty, it detaches from the orbiter and burns up in the atmosphere as it falls toward the Indian Ocean. It is the only part of the shuttle that is not recycled. The orbiter, which is about as big as a DC-9 jetliner, weighs over 20 tons with a cargo and crew of up to seven astronauts aboard.

It takes muscle to lift a heavy bird like that, and that power is provided by rockets. The orbiter's main rocket engines, used for lift-off, are not only powerful, but are the most complex rocket engines ever built!

Two minutes after blast-off, the white-hot solid rocket boosters separate from the shuttle and parachute into the Atlantic Ocean 30 miles below (left). They are picked up and reused. Once in orbit, the two orbital maneuvering system engines, located in the orbiter's tail pod, can be fired to change orbit or to take the spacecraft out of orbit for return to Earth. When the engines are fired, they cause a "burn," which can be seen behind the shuttle's vertical tail (right).

The front part of the orbiter is where the crew lives and works. It has two parts: the upper flight deck and the middle deck. The upper flight deck, or cockpit, has observation windows and controls; this is where the commander and pilot work. The middle deck is the area where the astronauts sleep, cook, eat, use the bathroom, and perform inside experiments. A pressurized airlock in the living quarters allows the spacesuited crew to exit and enter the spacecraft.

Trainees prepare for "launch" in the flight deck of Space Camp's mock-up of the shuttle *Columbia*.

A flight deck below the crew's living quarters houses life-support equipment such as water pumps and air-purification systems. These units make it possible for as many as seven astronauts to spend ten days in orbit.

The central part of the orbiter is the payload bay, which, at 15 feet in diameter and 59 feet in length, is big enough to hold a Greyhound bus! Payloads such as satellites and scientific experiments are carried here. A robotic arm, named the remote manipu-

Challenger, launched on June 18, 1983, coasts in a near-circular orbit around the Earth at a speed of nearly 17,500 miles per hour. Its payload doors are wide open and will remain open throughout the mission to keep the orbiter from getting too hot. In the open payload bay are satellites in protective pods, ready for launching.

lator system (RMS), is fixed to the left side of the bay. Created by the Canadian Space Agency, it is used to help astronauts capture and work on satellites that need repair, or to work on repairs to the shuttle itself. Two doors on the bay, which are opened once the shuttle is in orbit, allow cargo or experiments to be exposed to space. Satellites and experiments can also be launched into orbit from the bay.

There isn't much room inside a shuttle. But the near-zero gravity, or weightlessness, of orbital flight allows astronauts to use every wall and surface of the cockpit and living quarters for work, sleep, and play. This makes it seem bigger. And there is always the chance to take a walk in space.

Columbia inches its way out of the Vehicle Assembly Building at Kennedy Space Center to make the long journey to the launch pad. The date is December 29, 1980. On April 12, 1981, astronauts John Young and Robert Crippen hurtled into space aboard the first space shuttle. A new era in space exploration had begun.

America's first space shuttle, *Columbia*, hurtled into space on April 12, 1981, with astronauts Young and Robert L. Crippen aboard. They circled 200 miles above Earth for 54 hours and then returned safely to Edwards Air Force Base in California. The age of the space shuttle had begun!

A string of victories followed. A series of successful flights launched communications and Earth observation satellites for businesses and for various countries. On-board scientists, called payload specialists, working inside the orbiter, performed experiments in zero gravity. And on June 18, 1983, Mission Specialist Sally K. Ride disproved any notion that only men should "man" a NASA spacecraft when she shot into orbit aboard *Challenger*. While the terms "manned" and "unmanned" are still used by NASA in a generic or "human" sense, nobody doubts that the many brave, highly trained women who have followed Sally Ride into space are true astronauts. Men and women have been learning to live and work together in space ever since.

Thanks to new rocket technology, they are free to do work outside as well as inside the shuttle. At first astronauts were tied to the orbiter by a lifeline during space walks so they would not drift away. Although a small hand-held rocket gun helped propel them around the spacecraft, they could never venture far from the home ship.

All this changed during the *Challenger* mission, launched February 2, 1984. Mission Specialist Bruce McCandless became the first person to spacewalk without a lifeline. Strapped into the rocket-powered manned maneuvering unit (MMU), the world's first human satellite flew freely in space. Using MMUs, astronauts can now leave the orbiter, jet over to a disabled satellite, and bring it back to the cargo bay for repair.

The success of the first twenty-four shuttle missions lulled people into thinking that spaceflight was safe. This idea was shattered by the explosion that blasted

Challenger out of the sky on January 28, 1986. The disastrous loss of all seven crew members set the U.S. space program back two years. Some people even called for an end to space travel because they felt it was too dangerous.

But the United States had traveled too far down the road of manned spaceflight to turn back. On September 29, 1988, America rocketed into space again with an improved, safer shuttle. NASA's five-orbiter shuttle fleet hasn't stopped since!

In the years since Young and Crippen first vaulted into space aboard *Columbia*, the United States has flown over fifty missions, each with special goals. Some missions carry technology developed by other countries into space. Scientific experiments are conducted by international crews of mission and payload specialists.

Communications, weather, and Earth observation satellites are placed in orbit. They help improve our lives and show us what we have never seen before. Through the eyes of astronauts and the lenses of space cameras, we have seen that our blue planet, Earth, is in danger. What we have learned has made us take steps to save our precious environment.

Other satellites have been launched to explore the solar system beyond our present reach. *Magellan* and *Galileo*, launched in May and October of 1989 by the space shut-tle *Atlantis*, are on two such missions. *Magellan* is mapping the planet Venus. *Galileo* is on its way to Jupiter.

New countries entering the space program bring fresh ideas with them. Already a second generation of shuttles—smaller, less expensive to build and run than the United States's pioneer fleet—is on the horizon. The European Space Agency (ESA) is developing a shuttle named *Hermes*. Japan plans to launch one called *Hope*. To move forward, NASA wants to design new spacecraft of its own.

"To launch these birds, we'll need new rockets," Danny says. "Maybe some of you will help design them!"

Astronaut Bruce McCandless flies freely in space. He is wearing the Manned Maneuvering Unit, or MMU, that allows him to jet away from the orbiter *Challenger* in the first untethered EVA in space history. It's February 7, 1984.

SPACE STATION FREEDOM AND THE FUTURE OF ROCKETS

After they eat lunch, Apple team has a free half hour before a Space Camp bus takes them to nearby Marshall Space Flight Center. There they will view the full-scale mock-up of Freedom's core modules, built by Boeing. As they try to decide how to spend the time, Danny catches sight of Konrad Dannenberg. He helped von Braun create the engines for the historic V-2 rocket as well as those for the Redstone and Saturn rockets, and is a favorite speaker of Space Camp rocketeers. Dannenberg is examining the park's latest addition—the Centaur, which is an upper rocket stage for Atlas.

Danny asks the engineer to tell the children about Centaur. This rocket stage helped boost seven unmanned Surveyor missions to the moon between 1963 and 1966. Surveyor explored and mapped much of the moon's surface before astronauts ever set foot on it. It also launched Mariner probes to Mars, two Pioneer missions toward the edge of the solar system, and the Pioneer-Venus mission.

Though Dannenberg's V-2 is part of rocket history, his mind is on the future. "There is so much to be done," he says. "We've only just begun."

He is pleased to learn that Apple team is on its way to see Freedom. "Good," he says. "Pay close attention. Someday one of you could be living on a space station."

"I don't know," says one trainee. "Some people say Freedom's too expensive. They think we should spend our money solving Earth's problems instead."

Another trainee shares what she has heard. "Some scientists believe we could explore space faster and better and learn just as much—maybe more—using robotic probes and satellites," she says. "They say that unmanned space exploration is cheaper, more efficient, and less complicated."

Dannenberg smiles. "Many fine people, including scientists, think as you do," he says. "But don't give up. The conquest of space won't be cheap or free of risk. The space station has been delayed because we have not been willing to pay the cost. But I believe that it *will* be built someday.

"And eventually we will venture farther into space. We may build a base on the moon. Someday we might even travel to the red planet, Mars, the planet most like our home planet, Earth. We will explore first with probes and satellites. We always have. But in the end, men and women will follow—just as astronauts followed the probes that first surveyed the moon. Space is the future...the new frontier. I wish I were your age again! I'd like to see it happen."

Rocket scientist Konrad Dannenberg explains to the Apple team how the Centaur upper stage rocket works.

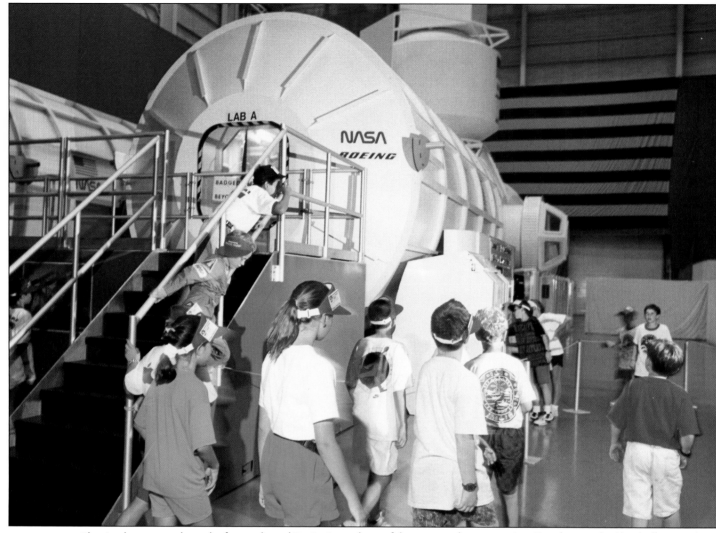

The Apple team explores the future aboard Boeing's mock-up of the proposed space station, Freedom, at the Marshall Space Flight Center in Huntsville.

Later, at Marshall Space Flight Center, the Apple team explores the model of Freedom. If a station like this might be built one day, they want to get to know it.

The station they see consists of several cylindrical modules, connected by passages called "resource nodes." The resource nodes contain command and control centers for space-station systems and communications. Two of the nodes have large viewing windows, where the crew could see and direct all activities outside the station.

The space station is supposed to be ferried up to space in sections by the shuttle. Once there it would be assembled by specially trained astronauts, using robotic equipment for assistance. In its present design, the modules are expected to be mounted on a long, horizontal frame. One module would serve as living quarters. The others would be laboratories, where scientific experiments would be performed.

Rocket thrusters, powered in part by solar energy, would keep Freedom orbiting around Earth. Astronauts would float freely in the zero-gravity atmosphere. Modules would be pressurized and kept at a comfortable temperature so men and women could work in normal clothes. Spacesuits would be used only for EVAs.

The design of Freedom would be based on Skylab. Floors and ceilings would be painted different colors; payloads and work stations would line the walls. This scheme would give the illusion of up and down, so the crew wouldn't get disoriented and spacesick.

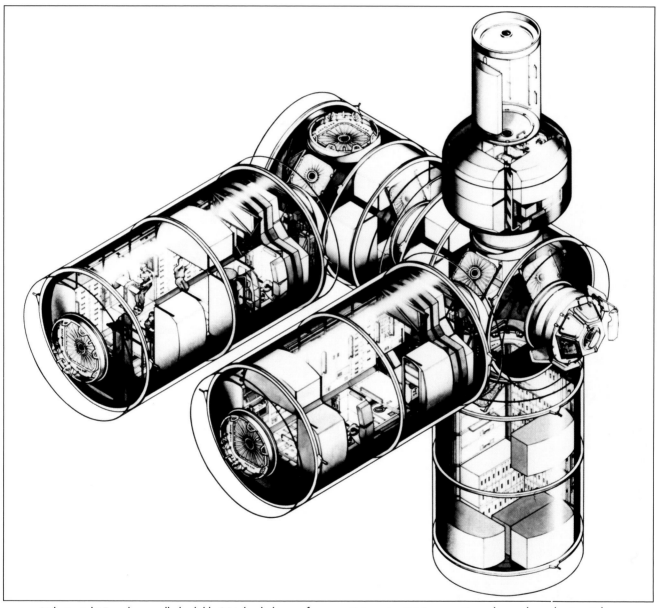

What might Freedom really look like? Nobody knows for sure. But most artists' conceptions show a long, horizontal metal frame with solar panels, communication dishes, and a central space station attached. This cutaway drawing shows one idea of the space station. There are four connected cylindrical modules where astronauts would live and work. Living quarters are in the top left module. The other three modules would house laboratories and work stations. The module at the bottom is a logistics module, where vital life support, electrical, and environmental systems would be stored.

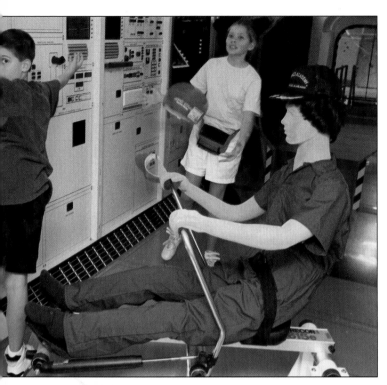

A rowing machine in Freedom's living quarters would let astronauts exercise every day. This would help prevent loss of bone and muscle mass during long periods of weightlessness. Special bathrooms, equipped with vacuum hoses, would allow them to take showers or to use the toilet without water or wastes escaping to float around the cabin.

A kitchen area, equipped with a microwave oven and tasty prepackaged meals and drinks, would give astronauts a good variety of food choices. Real ice cream might be available! CDs and videos would entertain them when they were not on duty. When they wanted to sleep, they'd attach their sleeping bags to straps on the walls.

On Freedom, everything possible would be recycled. Air, and even water from perspiration and urine, would be cleaned, sterilized, and used over and over. Only the space shuttle, or perhaps a space plane of the future, would be able to resupply Freedom with what its crew needed from Earth. Recycling wouldn't be a choice—it would be essential.

Small laboratory cubicles, fronted by transparent plastic doors equipped with special gloved openings, would be used for hands-on experiments. Astronauts would place their hands into the gloves and work inside the boxes without opening the doors. This would prevent tools and materials from escaping and floating around the lab. Experiments needing the vacuum of space could be stored in special compartments outside the pressurized modules.

As the trainees explore Freedom, they hope it will be the next step in the space program.

"It's a neat place, isn't it?" agrees Danny. "Before we return to the moon or make a trip to Mars, we *must* learn how men and women can adapt safely to long-term life in space. A station like Freedom might be a good place to do that. Many people believe it will be the first step in a bridge to the stars!"

The children leave Freedom excited about the future. One of them asks Danny, "What about rockets? We forgot about them while we were at the space station."

"No way!" Danny answers. "Rockets are more important now than ever. Spacefaring nations are already working on better, cheaper, expendable rockets to launch the probes and satellites of the future. We'll need a heavy launcher to hurl bigger payloads into space if we begin the space station, or start transporting tons of material to build a permanent moon base.

"Rockets like Redstone, Jupiter, and Saturn V were great in their day. But the space program outgrew them. While old rockets like Titan and Atlas are still used, it's time to move on."

Trainees explore Freedom. Daily exercise on the rowing machine helps keep astronauts fit *(top left)*. Computers *(top right)* and the remote manipulator arm inside one of the laboratory glove boxes *(bottom)* are fun to operate.

For manned missions to Mars and beyond, much more powerful rocket launchers would be needed. The weight of food, supplies, and life-support equipment necessary to keep a crew alive during a three-year Mars mission would make the spacecraft far heavier than the Apollo vehicles, which carried astronauts to the moon. The longest Apollo mission lasted only 10.5 days. A Mars mission would be more than 1,000 days longer.

However, once a spacecraft of this size and weight was launched—with sufficient speed so that Earth's gravity could not pull it back—no more force would be necessary to keep it moving forward. Special low-thrust rockets would be used only to make the ship go faster, to alter its course, or to help it land or take off from a planet.

New lightweight material for rocket construction would need to be developed to reduce weight and allow more room for astronauts and equipment. Smaller, more sophisticated computer and communications systems would be invented to guide spacecraft on their way.

The challenges for rocket scientists today are as vast as space itself. The combined efforts of the best minds in the world will be needed to solve them.

Even the shuttle, originally intended to be the air bus between Earth and Freedom, may soon become obsolete. A single shuttle mission can cost up to $500 million. If people are to travel back and forth in space, the cost of space travel must be reduced.

One answer might be an aerospace plane, like America's NASP (National Aerospace Plane). It would launch like a shuttle, fly through Earth's atmosphere as well as space, and land like an airplane. It would carry many passengers. Still on the drawing board, it looks more like a sleek, supersonic passenger jet than the sturdy shuttle.

The National Aerospace Plane would blaze a new trail in space flight history. One goal of the NASP is to make space travel less expensive and more available to ordinary people.

That night Apple team reflects on all they've learned about rockets and space. They file across Space Shuttle Park thinking about the space movie they've just seen, *The Dream Is Alive*. It is dark and still.

Suddenly the moon breaks through the clouds, casting a glow across the park. The shuttle flashes white against the blackened sky.

The trainees stop in their tracks.

"The dream *is* alive," whispers one. "Look at that!"

"Yes, it is," Danny replies with a smile. "Space is calling. Are you ready to go?"

Bibliography

In addition to numerous NASA publications, such as the *Report of the 90-Day Study on Human Exploration of the Moon and Mars*, November 1989; *Space Station Freedom: Gateway to the Future*, October 1992; and *Former Astronaut Biographies*, updated July 1992; the following books were particularly helpful:

Alabama Space and Science Exhibit Commission. *The Space Camp Staff Training Manual.* Rev. ed. Huntsville, AL: The Space and Rocket Center, 1989.

Asimov, Isaac, and Frank White. *Think About Space.* New York: Walker and Company, 1989.

Booth, Nicholas. *The Encyclopedia of Space.* New York: Mallard Press, 1989.

Embury, Barbara. *The Dream Is Alive: A Flight of Discovery Aboard the Space Shuttle.* Toronto, Ontario: Somerville House Publishers, 1990.

Kerrod, Robin. *The Illustrated History of Man in Space.* New York: Mallard Press, 1989.

Life in Space. Alexandria, VA: Time-Life Books, Inc., 1983.

Ordway, Frederick I., and Randy Lieberman, eds. *Blueprint for Space: Science Fiction to Science Fact.* Washington and London: Smithsonian Institution Press, 1992.

Rycroft, Michael, ed. *The Cambridge Encyclopedia of Space.* Cambridge, MA: Cambridge University Press, 1990.

The Software Toolworks Illustrated Encyclopedia. Novato, CA: Grolier, Inc., 1990.

Von Braun, Wernher, Frederick I. Ordway, and Dave Dooling. *Space Travel: A History.* Rev. ed. New York: HarperCollins, 1975.

Winter, Frank H. *Rockets into Space.* Boston: Harvard University Press, 1990.

Index

LAKE COUNTY PUBLIC LIBRARY
INDIANA